BLOCKCHAIN

The Technology Revolution behind Bitcoin and Cryptocurrency

by

Devan Hansel

Get the FREE Bonus NOW!

If you're interested in receiving free PDFs on latest updates and tips about stuff like blockchain, cryptocurrency, online trading, investing, real estate, stock market etc., I highly recommend you to join my list. I've spent many years understanding all this stuff and I will provide you the distilled knowledge that is most valuable to save your time.

Members in my list get to learn how to make money and invest it wisely. As a bonus, members will also be getting my latest books for FREE before anyone else. Yes, FREE. It's an exclusive list and the link to join can be found below. It doesn't cost you anything to join. You will only have to put in your email-id so that I can connect with you and keep you updated. It's a clear win-win. So, go ahead and subscribe now.

www.bit.ly/devan-hansel

Note to the Readers

Research studies have shown that 42% of people never read another book after graduating from college. So, I'd like to commend you for actually following up on your curiosity by getting this book. Given the public interest and rising market valuation of blockchain-based cryptocurrencies, this book is expectedly a smart and timely purchase. The value of cryptocurrencies has skyrocketed since their inception back in 2009 with Bitcoin. A window of opportunity has opened up for those who are interested enough to learn and brave enough to invest. Make no mistake, there is a lot of wealth to be made in this field. 2 years from now, people will look back and wonder why they didn't get on the boat while they still had the chance. The fact that you've bought this book indicates your interest. But are you willing to seize the opportunity?

A lot of time and effort has gone into creating the book you are now reading. And I sincerely hope that it helps you move ahead in your quest for knowledge. The book has been designed to take you gradually through the hoops and introduce the blockchain landscape, one block at a time. As such, care has been taken to ensure that anybody can read and understand the material without too many prerequisites. The book has also been written in a short-and-concise format so as to allow readers to flip through the book quickly. However, if you happen to find it difficult at times, please go through the resources recommended within the context. Good Luck!

About the Author

Hi there! I am Devan Hansel. I'm an investor with a technology background. Over the years, I've acquired a wide range of experiences in investing and the art of money-making by getting involved in the stock market, real estate, startups and more recently...cryptocurrencies and blockchain. Having studied computer science in college, I could easily grasp the essence of the blockchain technology and understand how the whole system works. In this book, I've laid out all the essential knowledge you need to understand how and why blockchain works the way it does. I've put my maximum effort in making it interesting and understandable. I hope you have a good time reading the book :)

Come join my list (www.bit.ly/devan-hansel) if you want to follow latest updates in the marketplace and get huge discounts on early releases of my books. All you need to do is enter your email-id so that I can communicate with you about my latest works and keep you in the loop.

Table of Contents

Chapter 1

Introduction to Blockchain

The term 'blockchain' has been thrown around more than a couple of times lately in the news, tech blogs and social media platforms. All this noise is bound to make us ask the question "Ok. What's going on here?". This book will answer all those basic questions like *What exactly is a blockchain? How can we use it? Are there any disadvantages or security threats?* and so on. If you pay close attention while reading these chapters, you will not only grasp the essence of the blockchain technology but also learn how to identify and invest in winning startups that are based on it.

But before we take a deep dive into the nitty gritty details, we have to step back and look at the big picture. This chapter will give you all the prerequisite knowledge required to make sense of the detailed chapters that follow. Among other things, you will learn about the history of blockchain and why it's so damn important in the near future. So, without further ado, let's get started.

Money & Currency

Let's start from the top. When two people have to exchange goods and services, they need a framework to assign value to what they want to offer/receive. This is where money comes in. Money is a form of value-representation. It is a system for assigning value that is recognized by the entities participating in the transaction. Without a mutual agreement, the concept of money is basically useless.

Over the years, people have developed different frameworks for assigning value like the Barter System, Gold Standard, Fiat currency. In the barter system, there was no standard for value-estimation. It was all left to the people participating in the transaction. For example, one apple could be exchanged for 2 bananas in one transaction and 4 bananas in another transaction. As the civilization progressed and more advanced trade started occurring, the governments decided to establish a *gold standard* for all transactions. Paper notes were issued which held value as enforced by the government. It was basically a guarantee that the government would issue the appropriate amount of gold in return for those paper notes. This meant that people could now trade and transact directly with the paper notes.

The Gold Standard was in effect for a very long period of time. It was only in 1971 that the U.S government led by President Nixon gave it up. Since then, every country has been using Fiat currency for financial transactions. Fiat currency is what most people think actual money is. It comprises of all the modern bank notes and the coins you see every day. Fiat currency is essentially the units of money minted, distributed and recognized by the government without a guaranteed return of gold for its exchange.

Most people think that money & currency are the same but it is important to identify the distinction between them. Here are some differences.

Money	Currency
1. Money is a medium of exchange. It is used	1. Currency is a system of monetary units. It represents

to measure and represent value.	money in physical/virtual form.
2. It is an abstract concept. There is nothing tangible about it.	2. Currency is real and tangible. It is the dollar bills and coins that you can touch and feel with your hands.
3. The amount of total money is fixed. Like the amount of gold in the world.	3. Currency can be created by printing notes or minting coins.
4. Money is highly durable and persists for a very long time.	4. Currencies rise and fall. They can be wiped out totally.

Digital Currency

Digital currency is nothing but money that is dealt with using electronic systems. This kind of money is also called *virtual money* or *cybercash*. Every unit of virtual money can be mapped to a memory block in some digital storage device like a hard disk. It is essentially stored and transferred over the internet using network servers and databases. There are many advantages to this type of currency. For instance, unlike physical transfer of cash which can be a hassle sometimes (risky, time-consuming, transaction fee etc.), digital transactions over the internet can not only be safe but also instantaneous provided the right software is used.

There are multiple forms of digital currency.

Virtual Currency is a digital representation of money which is purely online i.e., it does not have a physical counterpart. It essentially consists of virtual assets (called digital money) that are not regulated by a central financial authority. So, the reach and usage is limited to specific online communities that accept it.

Cryptocurrency is a digital currency in which the money is stored, transferred and verified using cryptographic techniques. It is also a virtual currency. The individual monetary units of the cryptocurrency (e.g., bitcoins) are created and safeguarded using complex cryptographic algorithms. Many cryptocurrencies are decentralized i.e., they are not controlled by a central bank or government authority. We will look into the effectiveness of cryptocurrencies in further chapters.

Advent of Cryptocurrencies

We've seen different systems for carrying out financial transactions rise and fall over the centuries. With the technology boom in the late 20th century, many people started exchanging goods & services on the internet. This called for a more robust digital financial system for carrying out secure payments online. This was the root cause behind the genesis of the cryptocurrencies that we see today.

Although many people have tried and failed to produce a high quality secure cryptocurrency framework, on October 2008, everything changed. A research paper was published under the pseudo-name of *Satoshi Nakamoto*. This paper was titled *"Bitcoin: A Peer-to-Peer Electronic Cash System"* and it introduced the world to a new kind of technology for carrying out online financial transactions securely.

Origin of Blockchain

The first sign of the blockchain concept came out in Satoshi Nakamoto's paper in 2008. Soon after, it was put into practice as a part of the bitcoin system. Although the initial purpose of blockchain was to serve as an underlying component of the bitcoin cryptocurrency, it received more public attention later on when people realized that the blockchain technology provided clear and effective solutions to two of the major problems faced in maintaining a secure distributed network. We will cover these problems and blockchain's solutions in chapter-3.

In short, blockchain is a distributed database for maintaining records. For cryptocurrencies like bitcoin, it is used as a public ledger for recording transaction details. The ledger is updated using specialized protocols that allow anyone in the network to validate transactions. Without this public ledger, the cryptocurrency would fall apart because there would be no effective way to distinguish valid transactions from the invalid.

Blockchain & Bitcoin

Although blockchain was introduced along with Bitcoin, it has since been adopted by lots of other cryptocurrencies. Each of these cryptocurrencies has its own purpose, benefits, transaction protocols etc. But almost all of them use the blockchain mechanism for keeping a record of the valid transactions.

Bitcoin was the first modern cryptocurrency to receive wide public acceptance. It was able to solve many hard problems that its predecessors couldn't. With Satoshi's solution, it was now possible to assign intrinsic value to digital artifacts (code essentially). And the technology that helped Bitcoin thrive as a cryptocurrency is Blockchain. It is important to distinguish between the two concepts.

Bitcoin is a peer-to-peer digital payment system with its own digital currency (also called bitcoin), wallet software and transaction protocols.

Although Blockchain was conceived as a part of Bitcoin, it is a separate technology unto itself. It is a mechanism that allows us to maintain a public list of valid records within a distributed network of mutually trust-less entities. We'll cover more of this in chapter-4.

Significance of Blockchain

Although blockchain was introduced along with Bitcoin, it has since been adopted by lots of other cryptocurrencies. Each of these cryptocurrencies has its own purpose, benefits, transaction protocols etc. But almost all of them use the blockchain mechanism for keeping a record of the valid transactions.

There are many properties of blockchain that make it highly desirable. Of those, immutability and distribution are notable because they solve the security problem that other financial systems haven't been able to, for centuries. Throughout history and up until recently, the only way to store value independent of any government's influence was physical materials like gold, silver etc. But with cryptocurrencies and blockchain, it has now become possible to do just that. Financial transactions can now be conducted independent of any central authority. This is quite a revolutionary breakthrough indeed.

Blockchain has undoubtedly led the way in transferring the power from large centralized banks and government financial organizations into the hands of the distributed public. It has made digital record-keeping safer, faster, cheaper and more elegant than ever before. It essentially cuts off the need for third-party entities and middle-men in carrying out verified online transactions.

The blockchain technology is in a relatively early stage (less than 10 years old). Venture Capitalists have invested more than 1 Billion dollars into this technology. This is an indication of the scope of development that is bound to occur. Below is a graph showing the increase in number of bitcoin's blockchain users over the years.

Blockchain has also been utilized in numerous other fields like the Stock Exchange, Gaming, Internet of Things(IOT), Supply Chains etc. It is generally considered to be an effective solution whenever and wherever it is required to deal with secure data transactions online.

The global community is slowly waking up to the benefits of blockchain technology. Every day, new companies and financial institutions are spending a lot of time and resources on implementing their own blockchain for various internal purposes. We will cover more about this in chapter-5.

The Cryptocurrency Market

Ever since Bitcoin came into existence in 2009, various other cryptocurrencies have been developed to address a plethora of needs. Many of them use the blockchain technology for dealing with the transaction records. As of this writing, there are over 900 cryptocurrencies that are in use. You can view them at *CoinMarketCap* which will also display the price, market capitalization and other details. Let's look at the top 5 cryptocurrencies currently in existence.

1. **<u>Bitcoin(BTC)</u>**: This is the first known cryptocurrency to be well-recognized and used by the public. It has paved the way for modern cryptocurrencies and is considered the de facto standard. Almost all the other cryptocurrencies have either branched off from or have major commonalities with bitcoin. It is currently the largest publicly traded digital currency. For a more knowledgeable guide on the technology behind Bitcoin and how you can profit from it by investing/trading/mining, check out my book "***<u>Bitcoin: The Digital Gold</u>***" on Amazon.

2. **Litecoin(LTC)**: Launched around 2 years after bitcoin, litecoin is a decentralized peer-to-peer cryptocurrency with a growing network of developers, merchants and supporters. Although very similar to bitcoin, it offers relatively faster transaction confirmations. Where bitcoin is gold, litecoin is silver.

3. **Ethereum(ETH)**: Launched recently (2015), ethereum is also a decentralized cryptocurrency but offers more functionality like *smart contracts*, the *ethereum virtual machine*, distributed computing etc. Currently, ethereum is the second largest cryptocurrency.

4. **Ripple(XRP)**: Ripple is heavily used by banks to settle global transactions in a secure and effective way at very low costs. It is different from bitcoin in its protocol and structure. Unlike bitcoin, ripple doesn't require high computing power for creation of new currency. As a result, it has a reduced network latency. The individual units of Ripple currency are called *ripples*(XRP). It is currently the third largest cryptocurrency in terms of market capitalization.

5. **Dash(DASH)**: Originally known as DarkCoin, Dash is also a decentralized peer-to-peer cryptocurrency like Bitcoin albeit a more secretive one. It was

launched in January 2014 and experienced a surge in traffic and fan-following quickly. Its famous features include instant transactions (*InstantSend*) and complete private transactions (*PrivateSend*). It also uses a separate chained hashing algorithm called X11 unlike bitcoin's SHA256.

<u>Note</u>: Cryptocurrencies other than Bitcoin are referred to as "Altcoins" because they are alternatives launched after Bitcoin.

As you must've already understood by now, the most promising and widely used cryptocurrency is bitcoin. A lot of reasons like durability, interchangeability, ease of transfer and scarcity make Bitcoin an exceptionally good cryptocurrency to invest in. If you're interested in buying/trading bitcoin while its price is still low, get an account at Coinbase. It is the most popular and reliable online exchange platform out there. Use the link below to get $10 OFF on your first purchase or trade of $100 or more. I use Coinbase myself for storing bitcoin and other essential base cryptocurrencies.

www.bookstuff.in/coinbase

But, where do cryptocurrencies get value from?

One of the original reasons cryptocurrencies were invented is to store digital assets securely and avoid interference from central powers like the governments and banks. Some cryptocurrencies are backed by gold and precious metals while others have no backing except the widespread acceptance by users. So, if there is no backing from the governments and everything is distributed globally, where do cryptocurrencies actually get value from and what are the factors influencing it?

1.**Supply and Demand**: One of most popular economic principles is the correlation of price of an object with its supply & demand. Let's take Bitcoin for example. As we've already covered, there can only be 21 million bitcoins in circulation due to the mining constraints. There are 7 billion people on this planet and as the adoption of Bitcoin as a global currency grows, there will be friction in the market caused due to growing demand and increasingly limited supply. This friction will lead to the rise in value of Bitcoin. It will also be amplified due to the fact that the popular strategy among many crypto-investors seems to be to "buy and hold". We will look at investing strategies in a later chapter.

2.**Mining difficulty**: Unlike fiat currencies which are minted by the national governments based on various monetary policies, cryptocurrencies are mined by volunteers. Mining cryptocurrencies requires a lot of electrical and processing power. And the cost is not getting any cheaper. So, the inherent difficulty involved in creating a unit of cryptocurrency leads to a certain perceived value. This goes up as the mining difficulty increases. Basic economics states that the price of something that is rare and valuable will be high. Many cryptocurrencies use POW (Proof of Work) protocol while mining new coins and validating transactions. And the POW protocol rewards miners who have spent more time and effort solving harder problems. This is a fair way to incentivize the miners and also ensure that there is a direct correlation between the price of the cryptocurrency and mining difficulty.

3.**User Requirements**: If a cryptocurrency has no practical benefits to users, how is it any good? The cryptocurrency has to solve user's problems to be considered valuable. This is similar to how a company's stock value will plummet if it's not delivering any good quality products/services to its customers. In addition to being a means of value exchange, many cryptocurrencies offer distinctive solutions to domains like legal contracts, digital security, Internet of Things etc. This makes the investors fund the project and the customers register and use it.

4.**Public Opinion**: This is one of the most underrated causes of price surges for not only cryptocurrencies but any other publicly traded stock/commodity. Despite what we may believe, a majority of people think emotionally and take decisions based on their gut. The term "panic selling" is famous among traders and investors. Any major news like a security breach or a market crisis will make the value drop. This happened in Feb 2014 when Mt.Gox, the most famous crypto-exchange at that time filed for bankruptcy as a result of cyber-attacks. When it comes to Bitcoin, a lot of people believe that the independent decentralized nature of currency will be more beneficial since it is less prone to corruption, fraud and manipulation by central banks and governments. The other side of the coin (no pun intended) is that there are also a lot of people who believe that Bitcoin is a currency used mostly by drug-dealers and criminals online. Nevertheless, the fact of the matter is that cryptocurrencies are blowing up globally and more people are becoming aware of the current crypto landscape and what it has to offer.

5.**Media & Law:** The price of a cryptocurrency can rise or fall depending on how the media portrays it to the public. There is always the possibility of getting blindsided by manipulative media. A few corporations or individuals who hold vested interest in a cryptocurrency can publicize its ICO (Initial Coin Offering) to bloat up its price in the market. This is why you should always do proper market research and look into a wide variety of sources including reddit forums, quora answers, facebook groups, google news/trends and multiple news and publishing articles. If you're tech-savvy, I would also advise you to delve into the source code and developer updates. Legal notices, Nation-wide bans and anti-cryptocurrency policies have also been observed in the recent past. Countries like China, Vietnam and Russia are active in their protest against public usage of bitcoin. This caused a temporary dip in the price of bitcoin but soon bounced back up to an all-time high. Meanwhile, many countries like Canada, UK, Australia are embracing the crypto-revolution and have provided infrastructure and policy support to the cryptocurrency communities. Some of them even have Bitcoin ATMs available across various cities.

6. **Investors**: The fact that a cryptocurrency startup has received funding from a good investor can boost

its coin price in the market. Investments are generally considered signs of trust. So, when a good/popular investor decides to put in capital for growing a cryptocurrency, a large portion of people decide to place their bets on it as well. Some malicious investors can also try to buy a large portion of the coins, inflate the price with press-releases or promotions and then sell them off quickly without any real progress. This is also referred to as the *pump and dump* strategy. The investors thus have a considerably high impact on the pricing of cryptocurrencies (especially altcoins with lower market caps).

7. **Market dilution**: With more than 1000 cryptocurrencies currently in the market and more coming in every year,

the market sure has gotten crowded with so many alternatives. Even if an innovative solution is offered by a brand-new cryptocurrency in the market, it doesn't take too long before a competitor opens shop with lesser token price and upgraded capabilities. This causes frequent and unexpected spikes in the prices of cryptocurrencies. Bitcoin, though, is considered a reserve cryptocurrency since it has the highest market cap and largest user-base, owing to its first mover advantage. Fluctuation in bitcoin price usually causes a ripple effect and creates a fluctuation in prices of other cryptocurrencies as well.

Chapter 2

The Blockchain Eco-system

In this chapter, we will sneak a peek under the hood of the blockchain technology and learn how all the individual pieces fit in together. Although the concepts have been covered in a relatively easy-to-understand manner, if you happen to find it a bit hard then make sure to follow up on the provided references and take your own time to understand the material. A mentor of mine once told me that learning is like eating steak. You don't try to gulp it down all at once. Rather, you cut it down into small individual chunks and take your time to chew them before ingesting.

That's how it goes with consuming knowledge as well.

So, what exactly is Blockchain?

Let us begin by asking the question – what do we need a currency for? Well, we need currency so that we can give it to others (buying) or take it from others (selling). Isn't this right? And for a cryptocurrency, that is where a blockchain comes into the picture. Blockchain is a technology that allows people to transfer cryptocurrency between one another securely. It is a distributed database where all the transaction records are saved. Unlike a typical fiat currency which is centralized, the blockchain of a cryptocurrency is distributed and spread across various countries and individuals. The databases and servers are run by volunteers who maintain a peer-to-peer network. There is no possibility of government or any third-party involvement in manipulating the database records. Even if the government officials or any malicious entities volunteer for maintaining the blockchain, they cannot alter the transaction records due to the constraints imposed by its design. Immutability is one of the biggest contributors of blockchain's success.

Blockchain is essentially an open electronic ledger where all transactions are recorded for public viewing. For example, the latest bitcoin transactions can be found at: www.blockchain.info. This open strategy of blockchain prevents counterfeits and other frauds. By checking the blockchain, you can be sure that the transactions are completely legitimate. Once you make a transaction, it will appear shortly on the public blockchain.

You might be wondering...*But won't people know who's spending how much by looking at the blockchain?* The answer to that is *No* because your identity is protected using encryption and mapping functions. Only your Wallet-ID will appear in the blockchain which reveals nothing about your personal identity. So, nobody can know for sure who you are and how much money you hold in your wallet.

The term 'blockchain' was initially used as two separate words *block* and *chain*. This is because the public ledger is stored and represented structurally as a chain of blocks. Each of these blocks holds a bunch of records. When new records that are validated have to be added, they are grouped into a block and appended to the blockchain. You will find below an image that depicts the skeletal structure of a blockchain. The black blocks constitute the main chain whereas the grey blocks are referred to as *orphan* blocks because of their lack of relevance (unfortunate naming, I agree). The white block is called the *genesis* block and it is the first original block to appear in the blockchain.

As you can see, the blockchain is not simply a sequence of valid blocks. If it were, it'd be called the blocksequence. But it contains multiple sub-chains as a part of the whole structure and later on, we will see why that is so.

Before we proceed, let's get any ambiguity in terminology out of the way. The scenario we'll be looking at is one in which there are a lot of "nodes" or computer servers in a distributed network. These nodes are not connected in any particular pattern i.e., their arrangement is haphazard. The word *blockchain* will refer to the structure of valid records (as represented in the previous diagram). Every node in the network will have its own version of the blockchain. And there is a public blockchain that represents the latest and most updated version. With this understanding, let's proceed to understand how a network like this can work consistently without any lasting disagreement on what is considered valid.

What is Mining?

Now that we have an idea of what the blockchain is, it is necessary to understand how it is updated unanimously throughout the network. It has to be unanimous because if the status of blockchain is not congruent among the nodes, it will lead to discrepancies in verifying transactions which will result in frauds and eventually, system failure. So, let's look into this in detail.

There are two kinds of nodes in a blockchain network. Normal nodes and mining nodes. Both of these have their own separate operating protocols. And every node maintains its own blockchain, constructed individually by adding valid blocks to the list. The normal nodes have relatively basic functionality. They receive messages containing transaction-data from neighboring nodes in the network. And their job is to verify the transactions and propagate them forward to remaining nodes. This will ensure that as time goes on, only verified transactions are spread across the network. This is a basic layer of security to ensure that bogus transactions are not updated in the blockchain.

Now, the mining nodes are a different kind of nodes. Mining nodes execute the mining protocol which is:

→ Listen for new transactions and verify them.

→ Aggregate verified transactions into a block.

→ Compute the solution to an algorithm called *Proof-of-Work* for that specific block.

→ Timestamp the block along with the computed *proof-of-work* value and broadcast it across the network.

The mining nodes essentially group new valid transactions into blocks and propagate them to other nodes. The validity of the block can be measured by any node by checking the *proof-of-work* value associated with the block. So, when this new block is received by the remaining nodes, they check its validity and add it to their own blockchain. A reward is given to the mining node that propagated the valid block with the earliest timestamp. This reward is usually a certain amount of the cryptocurrency units like bitcoins for example. It is similar to the processing fee charged by banks and other financial organizations.

Proof of work

The general idea behind this system is that creating a valid block is hard but verifying it is easy. The difficulty in creating or "mining" a valid block will make sure that there are not many spammers or freeloaders trying to update the blockchain with their own blocks. That's literally why this system is called Proof of work – you can only update the blockchain when you've actually done the necessary computation and can show your proof of work.

Let's take Bitcoin as our reference cryptocurrency. It uses a cryptographic hash function called SHA256. If you're not sure what that is, a cryptographic hash function is something takes any data as input and converts it into a random output that has no identifiable correlation with the input. So, any two similar inputs will have very dissimilar outputs. And calculating the input corresponding to a given output is next to impossible. As the name suggests, SHA256 is a cryptographic hash function that converts arbitrary sized inputs to outputs that have a size of 256-bits or 32-bytes. It was originally developed by the National Security

Agency(NSA) of America. Cryptographic hash functions are very useful in identifying data-tampering. They are used as one-way locks in many scenarios. And with blockchains too, they are used for a very similar purpose.

To prove that they've done the work, mining nodes have to compute the hash outputs of running SHA256 over the input containing, among other things, the transactions and a random number (called nonce). The hash output for a given input will always be the same. So, as the nonce (short for "number used once") changes, the hash output also changes. The mining nodes keep changing the nonce and calculate the hash outputs. When the output matches certain criteria, say having 10 consecutive zeroes in the beginning, the mining nodes have found the *proof-of-work* solution. They timestamp it and propagate the newly mined block of transactions to the network. When other nodes receive this block, they take the nonce and compute the SHA256 hash output of the transactions along with it. If the computed hash matches the criteria (10 zeroes in the beginning), the block is accepted and updated to the blockchain.

While computing the proof-of-work solution for a block, the mining nodes have to include the hash of previous block in their input. This ensures that the record of all the previous transactions stays intact. So, any node could take a valid block in the blockchain and calculate all the transaction history that preceded it. This lets the network check for invalid transactions and track the ownership of the cryptocurrency at any given point of time.

The mining process consumes a lot of computational power. Miners use specialized ASIC chips that are designed for calculating hash outputs. Miners also join their resources together into a mining pool to increase their probability of mining valid blocks. The Bitcoin system has been designed in such a way that it takes approximately 10 minutes for a new block to be mined by the mining pools on average. This difficulty is adjustable based on the criteria used for selecting valid blocks. For example, you could decrease the target number of zeroes in the hash output from 10 to 3. This will increase the difficulty of finding a proof-of-work solution and also the time to mine a new block on average.

The Dual-Purpose of Mining

So, now we know how blocks are mined, how the blockchain is built and how the *Proof-of-Work* protocol helps in making sure that every node on the network is on the same page. Here's the interesting bit. In most cryptocurrencies (including Bitcoin), mining is the only way to create new crypto-coins. That is to say, the only way for the system to assign value to the cryptocurrency is to measure the amount of computation performed by the mining nodes. Every bitcoin ever "minted" has been the result of a mining node performing the *Proof-of-Work* algorithm to create a new valid block.

The purpose of mining is twofold. To create new cryptocurrency and also update the blockchain with valid transactions. The reason that miners are rewarded is to incentivize them to perform the needed computation. If there was no reward, there wouldn't be enough miners to validate the transactions quickly. This would lead to a relatively unsafe system due to its high latency. The efficiency of the cryptocurrency depends on how fast the transactions are verified. And that depends on how many miners are competing for the reward simultaneously. This is the beauty of the bitcoin-blockchain system design. Also, the reward for mining goes down by 50% every 4 years for the bitcoin system. Eventually, there would be no reward for mining blocks except for the transaction fee and tips left by the users to the miners. This is a way to limit the supply of cryptocurrency and ensure that its value doesn't go down below a certain point.

The Blockchain is the heart of most cryptocurrencies. It is the bedrock on which all the transactions, security and efficiency of the system rely upon. Moreover, the tech community across the globe is waking up to the ingenuity of the blockchain design. Numerous applications of the blockchain technology are being identified in all areas of the digital spectrum. It may as well be that we've stumbled upon the backbone of a new kind of internet. If you're interested in getting latest market updates and FREE books, guides and tutorials, subscribe to my list below. I'll make sure you're well informed about significant technology changes and also investment opportunities.

www.bit.ly/devan-hansel

Hopefully, this chapter gave you the basic idea behind how the whole blockchain framework is set up. We've learned a lot of concepts in this chapter including mining, cryptographic hash functions, proof of work, the blockchain structure etc. In the next chapter, we will learn how this whole framework works in union to solve the two biggest problems facing any cryptocurrency.

Chapter 3

Solutions offered by Blockchain

In the last two chapters, we've looked at an introduction to blockchain and various elements that comprise it. We've understood that blockchain plays a key role in making a distributed network work safely and efficiently. It is a fundamental paradigm shift that has the potential to revolutionize the internet and many other prominent industries. In this chapter, we will look under the hood and understand how blockchain's solutions actually work.

Currently there are two major problems faced by distributed networks and cryptocurrencies. And they are, achieving decentralized consensus and stopping double spending. In the following pages, we will look at them closely to learn what the problem exactly is and understand how blockchain goes about solving them.

How Decentralized Consensus Works

The architecture of the blockchain is such that it eliminates the need for a central database or monitoring authority. You have to understand that this is a groundbreaking technological revolution not only in the field of digital currency but also in business, banking, governance, politics etc. A plethora of possibilities have opened up after it has been proven that a system like Bitcoin can be developed which achieves decentralized consensus in a secure and efficient manner. New self-verifying systems and decentralized apps are being developed today on account of this innovation.

To those who are unaware, decentralized consensus is when a network of entities comes to a common agreement about something (in the case of cryptocurrencies, the validity of a transaction) without having to trust one another. This is also known as distributed trust-less consensus and is a major research topic in the broader field of Distributed Systems. Many algorithms have been designed to solve this problem of distributed consensus. Cryptocurrencies like Bitcoin use a specific protocol called *Proof of Work* (POW), as we've seen, which lets the blockchain network achieve distributed consensus and operate without getting tampered. It is important to understand why achieving distributed consensus is so important in the first place.

Let's assume that you have a network of computers (also referred to as "nodes") that are interconnected in a haphazard manner. This network forms the *backend* of your service. In other words, all the computation and database storage operations are handled by this network *behind the scenes*. Your objective is to ensure that when a user performs an action, it has to be recorded and updated congruently throughout the network. So, your network is distributed but you have to project a single consistent experience to users everywhere. This is the most basic requirement for not only a cryptocurrency like Bitcoin but also for almost every big technology company out there like Google, Facebook, Amazon, Microsoft etc.

When a user performs an action, you will notice that in order to achieve the objective of consistency, you are inevitably left with only two options. Either record this action in all the nodes or none of the nodes. If you record it in only some of the nodes, there is an inconsistency in the network and the nodes cannot figure out the truth i.e., whether the user did actually perform the action or not. In other words, the network cannot come to an agreeable consensus. This is a big problem because an inconsistent network is an insecure network. Any hacker would be able to exploit this inconsistency to spread viruses or manipulate the database to his/her advantage. Therefore, it is important for a distributed network to maintain consistent data across all nodes and be able to identify erroneous and inconsistent records quickly. This is the reason why distributed consensus is so important in a blockchain network.

Now let's look at how exactly the blockchain aids in achieving this decentralized consensus. We will be considering Bitcoin as the reference cryptocurrency.

Decentralized consensus in a blockchain is truly amazing. This is because all the nodes in the network are able to agree on the validity of a transaction without having to trust anyone else or knowing the identity of parties involved. That is why it is also known as trust-less decentralized consensus. If nodes in the blockchain network could trust at least a few other nodes then the protocol would be different. But as it happens, in a completely distributed decentralized network run by volunteers around the globe, we have no option but to assume trustlessness.

Decentralized consensus in a cryptocurrency using blockchain is achieved in an emergent manner. What this means is that there is no single point of time at which all the nodes in the network are able to agree on the validity of a transaction. As time progresses, more and more nodes will be able to arrive at the same conclusion. And this does not cause any harm to the network.

There are four phases in which this emergent distributed consensus is achieved. Let's look at them closely.

Remember that achieving distributed consensus means that all the nodes end up with the same set of valid transactions over time.

Phase #1: Verification of every incoming transaction by every node.

The nodes in the network receive data regarding various transactions from their neighboring nodes. Some of these transactions are just invalid. So, as a primary rule, all the nodes check the incoming transactions and collect the valid ones into, what is called, a *transaction pool* or *mempool*. The transactions are verified using cryptographic techniques based on a list of criteria that are public.

And this pool of valid but unconfirmed transactions are propagated across the network by each node. So, all the invalid transactions are weeded out by the nodes in the network.

Phase #2: Mining nodes accumulate valid transactions into blocks.

Mining nodes, as we've seen in Chapter-2, are special nodes in the network whose job is to collect valid transactions from their neighboring nodes, put them in a block and compute a value (*Proof of Work*) for the block. The mining nodes keep track of the latest blocks and compete with each other to create new valid blocks. These new blocks contain valid transactions with the appropriate *proof-of-work*. And then the blocks are propagated across the network to other nodes.

Phase #3: Nodes receive and verify blocks

As the nodes in the network receive blocks from various mining nodes, they calculate their validity. Anybody can accumulate transactions into blocks. But the trick here is that computing the correct *proof-of-work* of a block is very hard and therefore it reduces the chance of a transaction fraud. Once the remaining nodes receive a mining node's block, they verify it against the *proof-of-work* and add it to their blockchain structure which they've been maintaining and updating so far. As we've seen in Chapter-2, the blockchain structure is essentially a list of chains of valid blocks, ordered by their timestamps.

Phase #4: Nodes eliminate irrelevant blocks

Every node maintains and updates its own blockchain. Nodes can receive multiple valid blocks by different mining nodes. So, how can they decide collectively as to which of the received blocks should be considered while extending the blockchain? This is where the proof-of-work value comes in handy. Different blocks have different proof-of-work values. The bitcoin protocol states that while selecting blocks, preference should be given to that with the highest *proof-of-work* value. So, if a node gets two different "valid" blocks, it will choose the one with higher proof-of-work value. And if they are also the same, it will maintain two separate sub-chains in the blockchain until one of them exceeds the other in the total cumulative *proof-of-work* value sum. It will then discard the sub-chain with the lower proof-of-work value sum. In a way, the nodes give preference to the sub-chain in which the mining nodes have spent more computational power because the *proof-of-work* value sum is a measure of the amount of computation done by the mining nodes.

The Double-Spending Problem

The concept of blockchain was first brought to light by the Bitcoin inventor, Satoshi Nakamoto. It was (and still is) considered a brilliant engineering design partly because it was able to solve what no other digital currency could, before that point of time, which is to *'Ensure that the cryptocurrency units cannot be spent more than once.'*

This is termed as the double spending problem.

Unlike fiat currency, the problem with a virtual currency is not the creation of the currency units but to maintain them. Anybody can come up with protocols/algorithms defining how the virtual currency units need to be created, how they need to be structured, what the size (in bytes) of each unit should be and so on. But the fundamental problem that any currency, especially a digital currency, needs to solve is *Double Spending*.

A *double-spend* is a scenario in which one unit of currency is spent in two separate transactions. This can be done by duplicating the unit itself or manipulating the record of transactions. In case of cryptocurrencies, this 'record' is the public ledger aka the blockchain.

A typical fiat currency solves the double-spending problem by deploying special techniques to print the cash and identify fake bills. The banks that deal with fiat currency transactions also take extensive security measures to prevent their databases (which hold all the transaction and account details) from getting hacked and hijacked. If the security of the bank's computer-network was compromised, the potential for damage is huge. With countless cases of bank frauds, hacking attacks and duplication of cash, it is evident that a fiat currency's solution to the double-spending problem is undoubtedly flawed.

So, how does a cryptocurrency like Bitcoin solve this?

Unlike a centralized fiat currency, a system like Bitcoin does not maintain "balances" of the individuals. It only maintains a ledger of transactions i.e., the blockchain. So, this issue is handled by assigning identifiers to bitcoins so that when someone tries to spend a bitcoin with the same identifier twice, it can be checked against the transactions recorded in the blockchain.

The way this works is, whenever you send someone bitcoins, that transaction is identified and recorded using a UTXO which is short for Unspent Transaction Output. This UTXO is the unique identifier that represents a transaction of bitcoins which is similar to a bill of fiat currency. UTXOs can be spent only as wholes. But they can be converted into multiple smaller UTXOs for transaction convenience.

When you want to spend some bitcoins, you have to either merge or split two UTXOs to create the new set of UTXOs you want. For example, consider that you have two UTXOs of 0.3 and 0.6 bitcoins, received from Alice and Bob respectively. Let's refer to these using their IDs, X and Y. So, X represents the UTXO of Alice and Y that of Bob. And let's say that you want to send 0.7 bitcoins to Carter. The conversion goes as follows:

X (0.3 bitcoins) + Y (0.6 bitcoins) => Z (0.7 bitcoins) + W (0.2 bitcoins)

Z and W represent the unique IDs of two new UTXOs created so that 0.7 bitcoins can be sent to Carter. Now, this new UTXO(Z) can only be spent when used in conjunction with Carter's signature. It is propagated across the network and eventually picked up by a mining node which hashes it into a block and updates the blockchain. That is how the transaction takes place. And the conversion is handled by a software called the *cryptocurrency wallet*. The other UTXO(W) worth 0.2 bitcoins goes back into your wallet and is spendable only in conjunction with your signature.

With this framework in place, all that a node has to do to verify if a bitcoin is being "double-spent" is to check the ID of the UTXO against the blockchain's transaction records. Even if a node's blockchain is incomplete, the faulty UTXO will get propagated only so far before getting dropped by the other nodes with complete blockchains.

Who maintains the servers and Why?

You must be wondering.....if maintaining and updating the blockchain takes so much effort, who would want to do this? Why would anyone want to volunteer for this kind of a thing?

The answer to that is *Mining incentives.* As we've already seen, most cryptocurrencies are designed in such a way that the people who validate transactions and update the blockchain are rewarded with new crypto-coins. This serves them as an incentive for their efforts. Rewarding the miners is the only sustainable way of maintaining a distributed decentralized cryptocurrency network. This is because mining the crypto-coins requires a lot of computational power provided by specialized GPUs and also involves paying a lot of money for electricity bills.

It also happens that in cryptocurrencies like Bitcoin which have this blockchain framework in place, mining is the only way of generating new cryptocurrency i.e., the new crypto-coins in the network are only generated when a miner creates a new valid block. This is a clever strategy to solve two problems in one shot. The miners get incentivized and the network gets new crypto-coins to work with.

It is very important for the system to be designed in such a way that **anybody** can come in and volunteer as a miner in the network. If the ability to mine was exclusive, the banks or the government or the top 1% wealthy corporations could find a way to attain too much control over the system. This could jeopardize the safety and smooth-sailing of the cryptocurrency. For example, if a bank was bombed and/or its servers were hacked, its customers would be in trouble. But with a widespread network of mining volunteers, there wouldn't be a single point of failure. This was something that Satoshi Nakamoto made sure of, while designing the system.

At this point, we have an understanding of how the blockchain works, the solutions it offers and why they're effective. But before we jump the gun and start implementing the technology or investing in it, we need to understand at the possible pitfalls and reliability issues. And this is what we will be looking into in the next chapter.

Chapter 4

Safety & Security of Blockchain

A cyber network is only as strong as its weakest link. With blockchain spearheading the revolution in cryptocurrencies and other fields, it is indeed quite important to understand exactly how vulnerable it is. So, if you're someone who's interested in getting the complete picture (positive and negative) before making an investment or if your company plans to get integrated with blockchain for increasing efficiency or if you're just curious, this chapter will be of some help.

There are mainly two types of blockchains. Public and Private. Both of them have their own pros and cons. We will cover them here in this chapter.

Public blockchain

A public blockchain consists of a totally distributed ledger which is maintained by the volunteers and there is no bias imposed on who can become a volunteer and contribute to the blockchain. The Bitcoin system uses a public blockchain. Although public blockchains support decentralization, the freedom to update the ledger from anywhere in the world has led to questionable usage scenarios. For example, Silk Road, an online black market, has been found to be operating with hundreds of thousands of bitcoins for illegal trading of drugs. This is one of the biggest drawbacks of having a distributed decentralized cryptocurrency. The NSA and FBI are actively involved in finding organizations and individuals who participate in such anti-social, illegal operations.

Private blockchain

On the other hand, a private blockchain is controlled by operators that manage the mining nodes and limit the power of updating the blockchain to certain specific nodes so that it doesn't go haywire. They achieve this by authorizing the nodes and controlling the network architecture. A well-connected node will have easier time updating the blockchain because it can transmit its mining-solution faster. In private blockchains, the ability to read the transaction-ledger is also limited by the operators. These private blockchains are slowly finding their place in various fields like land registries, trading platforms, private equity funds etc. One of the security concerns when managing a private blockchain is that if the major nodes (widely connected) find themselves offline, there will be a lot of transactions that remain unverified and un-updated in the blockchain. This will lead to inconsistency and inaccuracy even after those nodes come back online. So, it is important to ensure that these "central" nodes have heavy backups and enough support to quickly come back online.

The main difference between public and private blockchains is the extent to which they allow decentralization and anonymity. Another type of blockchains called "hybrid blockchains" also exist which are essentially in the middle of the spectrum with partial decentralization. They also have similar properties and drawbacks as the other two types.

Other security concerns of blockchain

1. **Irreversibility:** Once made, transactions in the blockchain cannot

be reversed or undone i.e., you can't erase an entry in the ledger forever. So, if you transfer your cryptocurrency to a wrong address, you can essentially kiss it goodbye because as long as the transaction is verified as cryptographically valid by the nodes, it will propagate across the network and be updated in the blockchain. You can only add transactions to the ledger, not delete them from it.

And also, loss of your private-key will result in loss of total cryptocurrency. Although the crypto-coins will be yours by right, you cannot claim them unless you have the private-key to prove it. Within the blockchain network, there are a lot of unidentified bitcoins floating around which nobody can claim because that's how the system/algorithm works. Estimated loss in bitcoin value due to this type of incidents is approximately $950 million. Your private key is your only source of identification in the network. If someone steals it, it is impossible for you to recover your bitcoins because the transactions made by the stealer that are recorded in the ledger are verified as true by all the other nodes. This is a price we must pay for choosing a decentralized distributed technology like blockchain. It works well so long as you don't lose your private-key.

Hey there! How's the reading coming along? I hope it's good and you're getting some useful knowledge. If you are, I want you to share your two cents by writing a quick review on Amazon. It won't take more than 2mins. But it will mean the world to me. I need your feedback. You can directly write the review by searching for "Blockchain" on Amazon or by visiting the link below. Thanks a ton!

www.bookstuff.in/blockchain-review

2. **Distribution of power:** If a malicious entity can somehow attain ownership of more than 51% of the nodes in the network, it will no longer be a fair system. This is called *The Majority Attack*. The attacker can dominate the network by only relaying some specific transactions and ignoring others. If this happens, the blockchain will be vulnerable to various other attacks as well. The ledger cannot stay incomplete

for too long. So, the best bet we can have is to ensure that there are more individual entities from different backgrounds volunteering for the blockchain. The power to update the blockchain HAS TO remain distributed.

3. **Latency:** In certain high-end financial systems where operational speed is critical, blockchain can become a bottleneck. The USP of blockchain is that it allows us to operate a network where mutually trust-less nodes can transact valid data. It is a self-correcting system but takes time to arrive at the truth because of the "trust-less" factor. As such, banks and other businesses trying to incorporate blockchain into their software solutions have to be

extra cautious of reducing the response time for their customers.

Despite these forthcomings, blockchain is still being used heavily in many of the core platforms online. It has millions of users around the world. Hundreds of thousands of people are working on developing this technology for the better. And that kind of attention from designers, engineers and experts is bound to create only better versions of the technology in the future.

Chapter 5

Applications of Blockchain

In the previous chapters, we've seen all the functionalities and limitations of blockchain. We've understood how its unique solutions work and where they might fall short. As the technology gets more popular, it is being updated and adapted into lots of different fields. And many industries are set for being revolutionized by the advent of blockchain. In this chapter, we will look at the most prominent of these areas where blockchain is being used as a solution.

1. <u>Cybersecurity</u>

The primary motive behind invention of blockchain technology was to enable a public ledger for a distributed decentralized cryptocurrency. Although it had a rather limited implication in Satoshi's original research paper, blockchain now finds itself being used heavily in environments where secure data transactions have to be made in distributed networks.

The fact that the bitcoin blockchain has stood firm against 8 years of numerous cyber-attacks is a testament to its robustness. In fact, a news article from cnet.com states that the world's biggest defense contractor, Lockheed

Martin, is now involved heavily in adopting blockchain for its cybersecurity solutions. According to the article, the VP of Lockheed Martin was quoted saying that these new blockchain cybersecurity methods will enhance data integrity, faster problem discovery and mitigation.

Companies like REMME are using blockchain to make user login-passwords obsolete. Their motto is *No more passwords – no more break-ins.* By assigning private SSL certificates to devices and managing them on a blockchain, REMME makes it almost impossible for hackers to bypass/crack the authentication.

As we've observed in the previous chapter, a cyber network is only as strong as its weakest link. And for many digital networks out there, the involvement of a human factor (security officer, admin, moderator etc.) creates almost all the vulnerability. By adopting a distributed ledger mechanism, the blockchain presents us with an innovative and effective security solution. With wide interest from all over the world including the U.S's Pentagon, it is becoming more and more evident that Blockchain will find itself a special place in the cybersecurity space.

2. <u>Voting Systems</u>

As we saw in chapter-3, one of the main solutions offered by blockchain is its ability to achieve distributed consensus. And what better application of that than in public voting. With a public ledger of votes made, voters can safely verify if their vote is being considered while remaining anonymous. This is a huge step towards 'e-democracy' to ensure an open and fair government.

The first ever country to apply this in real elections was Denmark in 2014. Blockchain-based digital voting systems were used for internal elections of a political party. And this can serve the rest of the world as a precedent in the adoption of latest technologies to meet the political requirements of the country. With many Americans still believing that elections are rigged and that there is a lack of safety & security, blockchain can come to the rescue and turn up the shockingly low voter count in the country.

3. <u>Banking & Finance</u>

Given that Blockchain was originally conceived to deal with financial transactions, it is no surprise to notice banks and other financial tech companies showing massive interest towards this distributed ledger technology(DLT). With proper network architecture and maintenance, private blockchains can offer very cheap and very efficient alternatives to banking solutions. Because of blockchain's ability to avoid being controlled by centralized power, it is used for international payments, remittances and other global financial services.

Due to the rising popularity of blockchain in the financial space, many banks and fintech (short for financial technology) organizations have either invested into or are collaborating with new blockchain-based startups. Banking goliaths like Goldman Sachs, Morgan Stanley have even published some research on this while others are building their own patented technology. A paper published at www.finextra.com titled "Rebooting financial services" found that integrating blockchain-based solutions can save banks up to $20 billion per year. That's some crazy savings!

4. <u>Supply Chains</u>

By maintaining a public ledger of all the transport records, we can create a lot of transparency between the consumer and the creator. Many problems related to customer-satisfaction can be avoided. For example, when someone receives a product, they will be able to look up the blockchain to know exactly where it got shipped from, who handled it in the middle and whether it's a fake or authentic piece. This will be a very useful feature to have when dealing with food and medicines.

5. Digital Identity

Imagine never having to worry about someone stealing your credentials or impersonating you online. The first step in many of the security systems is proper authentication of individuals. It is a precursor to access control i.e., your privileges and control capabilities will be assigned based on your authenticated identity. This is a major cause of security breaches and online frauds. There are thousands (if not more) of man-in-the-middle attacks and eavesdropping cases occurring every day.

Unlike the traditional systems which have a central authentication platform based on your login credentials, the blockchain network will arrive at a distributed consensus of whether your identity is valid or not. Blockchain-based identification methods will be irrefutably secure just like the way bitcoin's transactions are. And since ownership of the private-key translates to ownership of the digital assets, this technology can be applied to authenticate people with passports, birth certificates, driving licenses etc.

6. <u>Smart Contracts</u>

If you've been in the crypto-market for some time, you must've already heard of the term "smart contracts". A smart contract is like a normal contract between two parties except it is digital and programmable. So, instead of relying on a third-party witness or the law, you can be safe to rely on the software code and the blockchain network to enforce the contract for you. This is basically an extension of the decentralization aspect of blockchain to the realm of legal contracts. Instead of having to trust a central authority, you let a decentralized network bind and hold the contract.

It's like automation of the legal system or at least a part of it. For example, if

Alice and Bob create a smart contract saying that if certain conditions aren't met by a particular date, Alice has to send $100 to Bob. This contract will be updated on the blockchain and as long as it's not changed by either Alice or Bob, the network will trigger the transfer of funds on the set date after checking whether the conditions are met. It's a simple clean way to make deals, bets and strict contracts. And it helps individuals and businesses bypass the painful legal and regulatory procedures required of normal contracts. In fact, there is an entire cryptocurrency based on this smart contract technology called Ethereum which is currently the second biggest after Bitcoin.

Chapter 6

Investing in Blockchain

First of all, I'd like to put out a disclaimer that I am not a professional investor and would advise you to consult a legal or financial advisor before you invest in anything based on what is mentioned in this book. The content here is only intended to throw some light on the blockchain landscape and provide you with mere guidelines when deciding to spend your time/money on it. So, with that out of the way, let's look into the methods behind the madness.

Investing in Blockchain Startups

Blockchain startups, from an investment standpoint, are like any other startups in the sense that if you invest in 10 blockchain startups, 8 of them will probably fail and the other 2 will probably succeed and return your investment by 200-400%. This is the general statistic behind most investment strategies. So, you should expect to hit very few home runs while the majority fail. Nonetheless, here are some factors to consider before making your investment.

1. **The Team**: First and foremost, you need to understand that when you decide to invest in a blockchain startup,

you are essentially deciding to give money to a certain group of people and not some random system or machine. What happens with your money will be mostly based on what that team does. So, you want to equip yourself with as much knowledge of the team as possible. How well do the founders understand each other? Are the employees competent enough? Do they seem like they have any internal disputes or do they actually like to work with each other? If you fund a bad team, your money will go down the drain. If you fund a good team, you might have a success. So, having a good team is one of the first pre-requisites for a successful startup. And as an investor, you need to spend a lot of time with the people before you spend any money on their startup.

2. **The Business Goals**: What problem does the startup want to solve? What customers do they want to serve? Why is it an important problem to solve? Is there any data to back this? How might this problem be irrelevant? You have to do your own market research to validate the startup's claim. And you also need to be educated about the domain in which the startup is operating in. When you're investing your money, getting blindsided is the least useful thing. So, you want to minimize its probability as much as possible.

3. **The Solution**: After you're convinced that the problem is significant enough, you need to hear the elevator pitch. If the startup's founders cannot express

their solution clearly in less than 5 minutes, you can assume that they will have a lot of trouble bringing it out into the world. The startup's vision should convince you of a better future. You don't want to get into business with people if you're second guessing their solution. So, make sure you're on the same page with the team as far as the big picture and roadmap are concerned.

4. **Timing**: Is the market ready for the solution? Too soon and you will fail to capture the market's attention. Too late and you will face a great disadvantage. This is why your market research is crucial. If the startup is tuned in with the market's needs properly, things will just fall into place.

As an investor and share-holder, you need to sense the market accurately and predict the best direction for the startup especially in the early stages. This is something that seasoned investors seem to figure out easily although that's not always the case. Gary Vaynerchuk, author, entrepreneur and investor, says that the best companies and organizations hack culture. They get a pulse of what is in demand before others and place their bets accordingly.

As an investor, you have to do the same and sadly there are no specific techniques that can be taught because if there were, everyone would be successful. All you can do to get better is spend a lot of time studying the market scene, latest products in the field and the news. I'd recommend you to join my list where you will get latest updates, opportunities and books on many topics related to investing, cryptocurrencies, real-estate, online trading etc. If you haven't already, go to the link below and subscribe.

www.bit.ly/devan-hansel

Investing in Blockchain ICOs

An ICO, short for Initial Coin Offering, is similar to crowdfunding where you can invest in a startup by purchasing cryptocurrency. The only difference is that the investor's prime interest is to get back profits and not necessarily to fund/control the startup. The startup will use this investment as capital to work on various projects and if it's successful, the value of the cryptocurrency will raise substantially. An example of a good ICO is the Ethereum project. It raised funds initially at $0.4 per ether and as of this writing, one unit of ether is worth around $311 and the total market cap of ethereum is over $29 billion.

The general idea is to invest in multiple blockchain ICOs and hit a home run with at least one that will cover the losses incurred with others and give additional returns. When you invest in, say, 10 ICOs, the likelihood of winning at least one of those bets is reasonably high. The win rate, as described by the cryptocurrency experts, is usually around 20%. This means that 2 out of your 10 ICO investments have a good chance of giving you 10X or more returns. As with blockchain startups, ICOs also need to be analyzed carefully. You need to research the project, its members, their backgrounds, goals, offered solutions etc. It's a lot of homework but for a profitable ICO, definitely worth the time & effort.

Arvind Krishna, IBM's Director of Research, said in an interview with Bloomberg on March 2017, "I believe that blockchain will change the physical world, not just the world of money." Given that big companies and venture capitalists are investing heavily into this technology and many new blockchain startups sprouting up every day, the opportunity available for a sensible investor is huge. Apparently blockchain will do to transactions what the internet did to information. So, if you follow the guidelines presented in this chapter and pay close attention to the market, you too can benefit from this revolution.

Chapter 7

Future of Blockchain

Blockchain has already been responsible for the spawn of the cryptocurrency era. The amount of wealth and convenience it has created with just Bitcoin is unbelievable. We will be seeing a lot more cryptocurrencies pop up in the future which will mean that we will have access to a lot more digital solutions in our hands – all thanks to Blockchain. With the kind of attention and resources being poured into developing this technology, we can expect it to grow into a giant backbone for all kinds of applications.

Here is a graph of the increase in bitcoin's blockchain wallet users over the last couple of years. Needless to say, the growth in user base has been outrageously high and is only bound to increase even more due to network effect.

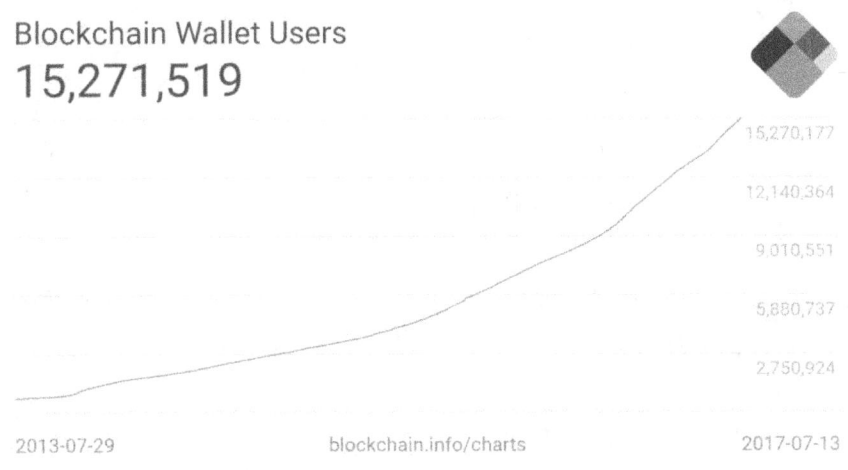

Blockchain Wallet Users
15,271,519

15,270,177

12,140,364

9,010,551

5,880,737

2,750,924

2013-07-29   blockchain.info/charts   2017-07-13

As things stand, we will also see blockchain at the forefront of finance, being used in almost all banks and fintech organizations to handle digital transactions. This will lead to billions of dollars saved as a result of improved efficiency and reduced infrastructure costs. You will find below a graph of the total number of transactions carried out by the bitcoin's blockchain in the last 2 years.

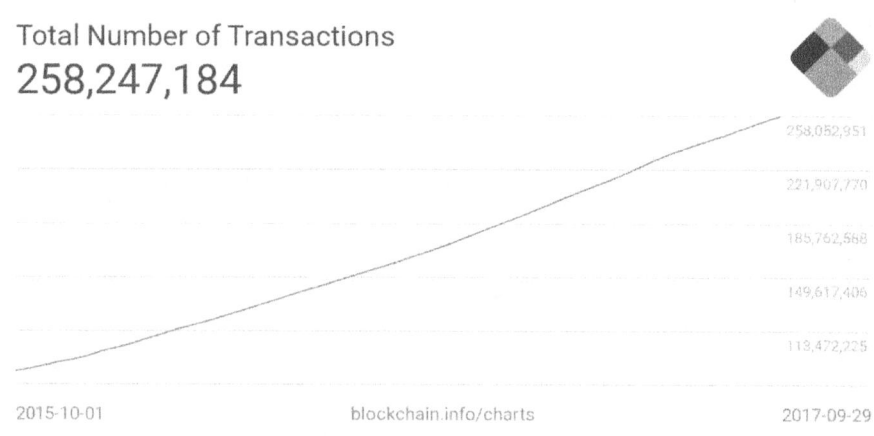

Total Number of Transactions
258,247,184

2015-10-01   blockchain.info/charts   2017-09-29

Meanwhile, here are some things that people from Silicon Valley (and around the world) are saying about the future of blockchain.

"The consequences of this[blockchain] breakthrough are hard to overstate."

- Mark Andreesen, co-founder of Netscape

"Blockchain is the next big unlock."

- Jack Dorsey, CEO of Twitter.

"I'm a big believer in the ability of blockchain technology to effect fundamental change in the infrastructure of the financial service industry."

- Bob Greifeld, CEO of NASDAQ

"Blockchain for identity is the core of the Internet of Things."

- Eric Jennings, Co-Founder of Filament

"Instead of putting the taxi driver out of a job, blockchain puts Uber out of a job and lets the taxi driver work with the customer directly."

- Vitalik Buterin, co-founded Ethereum

Ameer Rosic, who maintains a YouTube channel on cryptocurrency and blockchain related technologies, points out in his videos that the main feature of the bitcoin-blockchain system is that it cannot be duplicated, replicated or manipulated.

Predictions of the Future & Blockchain

Although it's impossible to predict very accurately, what the future of this tech space will look like, we can at least attempt to guess or imagine the possibilities. Here are some popular predictions made by various online communities and experts about how this technology and its impact will look like in the coming years.

1. **Eliminating the middle man**: You must've already understood by now that the USP of blockchain is that it validates transactions in a mutually trust-less network. As such, it has the potential to eliminate the "middle man" in all sorts of product/service

oriented transactions like real-estate deals, art deals, recording contracts, investments etc. As a result, there will be little or no gap between the seller and the buyer.

2. **Smart Contracts:** This is currently being implemented with the Ethereum project. With programmable digital contracts, there will be a massive shift in the way business and day-to-day financial transactions are carried out. There will also be a huge impact on legal enforcement of rules/contracts for services/products that can be digitized. For example, if you sign a smart contract to rent an apartment and if you fail to pay the rent within due time, the power and utilities can be cut off automatically by the contract.

3. **Revolutionize Security:** Blockchain will be used to confirm/validate almost any important fact online. It will serve as an indispensable tool in not only digital voting systems but also in high-risk security systems for proper authentication of individuals and access control.

4. **Advanced IoT:** IoT (Internet of Things) consists of a group of devices connected typically over a private network that work together in automation. It got a boost in usability after the cloud technology came into light. There will be an estimated 20 billion devices connected over the internet by 2020. With so many devices interconnected, there is a big risk of

viruses and other cyber-attacks overwhelming the network. According to an article on networkworld.com, blockchain has the capacity to provide a reliable platform for IoT devices to operate on, without having too much concern with security and maintenance. The IoT network will essentially run on a private blockchain and can be operated remotely.

5. **Wide adoption in Finance:** Central banks will probably be the most-effected entities in the upcoming blockchain revolution. A majority of the online transactions will be carried out over public/private blockchains using cryptocurrencies. The future of banks and financial organizations will depend on how quickly and how effectively

they adopt the blockchain into their own systems.

In conclusion, I'd just like to state once again that blockchain has a major role to play in the coming years. The growth of economy and internet technology will only add to blockchain's impact. In no less than 10 years, we will have the ability to hook up any digital device to the blockchain and verify ownership and transactions of all sorts. And in no less than 5 years, blockchain will transform from being the "next big thing" to "the big thing".

One Final Word

Congratulations! You've made it to the end. Hopefully, it's been a fun and educational experience. I've certainly had a blast preparing this book for you. And once again, I want to express my deepest gratitude to you for having given me your time and attention. I hope you found great value worth your investment. If you did, I want you to just do this ONE thing for me.

Please leave an honest review on Amazon at the link below. That is the only way for me to get your feedback and improve my craft. Thanks a ton!

www.bookstuff.in/blockchain-review

More books from the author

Cryptocurrency: The Essential Guide to Understanding Bitcoin, Blockchain and More!

Cryptocurrency Trading: How to Make Money by Trading Bitcoin and other Cryptocurrency

Bitcoin: The Digital Gold